SUPER-CHARGED SCIENCE PROJECTS

ELECTROMAGNETS IN ACTION

NOTES

To Parents: Some activities in this book may require the guidance and supervision of an adult to insure the child's safety in handling certain cutting tools suggested for use.

About the Measurement Units Used: Both the U.S. system and the metric system are used in this book. However, the units are not exact conversions. They are approximations, to make measuring easier regardless of what system you use.

THE DEVICES YOU ARE GOING TO MAKE USE BATTERIES

NEVER TRY TO CONNECT THEM TO THE WALL OUTLETS!

YOU COULD CAUSE A SHORT CIRCUIT AND, WORSE STILL, YOU COULD GET HURT.

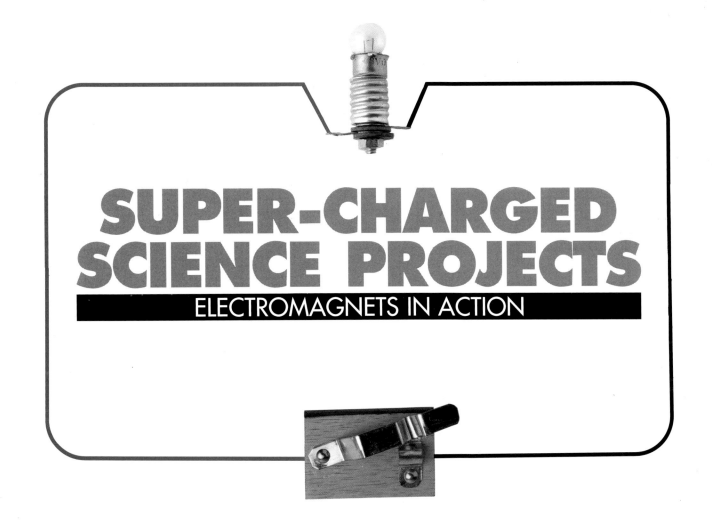

SUPER-CHARGED SCIENCE PROJECTS

ELECTROMAGNETS IN ACTION

BARRON'S

THIS IS <u>NOT</u> A SCHOOL BOOK!

There's no need to worry: There aren't any formulas or calculations to do.

We only want you to try your hand at carrying out these activities, all of which you should enjoy greatly.

So, ARE YOU READY FOR A CHALLENGE?

Of course you are. You learn new things better by playing, don't you?

The title of the Spanish Edition is *¿Te Atreves? Electroimanes en Accion*
© Copyright 1994 by PARRAMON EDICIONES, S.A.
Published by Parramón Ediciones, S.A.,
Barcelona, Spain.

Author: Parramon's Editorial Team

English translation © Copyright 1994 by Barron's Educational Series, Inc.

All inquiries should be addressed to:
Barron's Educational Series, Inc.
250 Wireless Boulevard
Hauppauge, New York 11788

Library of Congress Catalog Card No. 94-72512
International Standard Book No. 0-8120-6437-2

Printed in Spain
4567   9960   987654321

CONTENTS

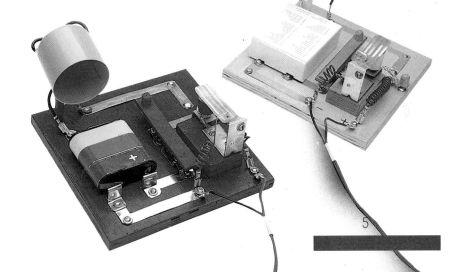

And keep in mind
that words in italics
that are marked
with an asterisk (*)
are explained in
the Glossary at the
end of the book.

5

INTRODUCTION

IT HAPPENED OUT WEST

You have, no doubt, seen many Western movies. And surely, in at least one of these films, the telegraph played an important role: The sheriff must send a message and the Indians, who don't want the message to reach its destination, cut the telegraph wire.

When you see any such scene, you can be certain that the story, real or imagined, happened after 1844. In fact, the first telegraph line, which ran between Washington and Baltimore, was inaugurated on May 22, 1844, by Samuel Finley Breese Morse. It worked by means of electric signals sent from a transmitter to a receiver, using a code that Morse invented.

The top drawing at right shows a bearded Samuel Finley Breese Morse (1791–1872). He was an excellent landscape and portrait artist, a founder of the National Academy of Design and Fine Arts, and a Professor at New York University. However, from a very early age he had a great interest in science and technology, which later made him abandon his teaching profession. He owes his fame to the invention of the electric telegraph named after him, and also to the Morse language system developed for the telegraph, based on dots and dashes.

The Morse telegraph made an enormous contribution to the development of long distance communication, especially after 1856, when Western Union united all the many small companies by using the Morse magnetic telegraph system. As you will soon see (after you've had a chance to play with the telegraph device you'll be making on pages 30–45), Morse's invention is one of those brilliant ideas that come once in a while: With the simple application of an electromagnet, Morse was able to convert electric impulses into sound or graphic signals, which, thanks to a code he invented, could be interpreted as letters of a normal writing system. Surely you've heard of the "Morse code," as it is called.

These days, electromagnets are common and in wide use, but Morse presented the first magnetic telegraph in 1837, merely nine years after the first electromagnets had been constructed.

The Morse telegraph not only contributed to the settling of the American West, within a few years, it also connected the entire Western world through an immense network of electric wires.

This book—which is entitled *Electromagnets in Action* because it is dedicated to the construction of devices whose function depends on an electromagnet—gives you the chance to recreate Morse's invention. With a little imagination, you may even feel like an actor in an old Western movie. More so if you and your brother or sister build a telegraph between two rooms in your house, or if you work together with a neighbor or friend to join your two houses with a telegraph. It's not hard to do.

The construction of the first major telegraph lines was a true adventure. Connecting America's East Coast and the then wild West through miles* of conducting wire mounted on wooden poles should really be considered one of history's epic feats.

BEFORE YOU BEGIN

LET'S TALK ABOUT TOOLS

We want you to have fun as you build a series of interesting devices. But we also want you to experience the satisfaction that comes from knowing that you have done a good job: Prove to yourself that with a little thought and some manual skills you are capable of building things that work. Of course, to do this you need tools.

From the beginning of time—as prehistoric people learned how to flake *flint** for making spearheads, stone knives, mallets, and stone axes—the tools that humans have developed and are continually trying to perfect have contributed to humanity's progress.

In this book, we ask you to saw, cut, drill, bend, and polish metal, wood, and other materials. Therefore, in addition to the tools we recommend in the following list, *please note that you will require the supervision of an adult when using any of the cutting tools, such as the hacksaw and the scissors.*

TOOLS YOU WILL NEED

The tools you see here are available for sale in most hardware stores.

1. Small flat-nosed pliers, used for holding and bending metal wires and connecting wires.
2. Long-nosed pliers, with a rounded nose to give a round shape to connecting wires and sheet metal pieces.
3. A small, inexpensive hacksaw. You need it for sawing iron rods and small pieces of wood.

4. A small awl.
5. A half-round file, which is flat on the other side.
6. A round file, the kind called a "rat-tail" file.
7. A small, flat-head hammer.
8. A vise.
9. Combination pliers, which have many uses: to hold and flatten wires and small pieces of metal (with the nose), to cut thin wire (with the metal clippers), to cut thick wire (with the side blade).
10. Electrician's scissors, or kitchen scissors.
11. A medium screwdriver.
12. A compass (not shown).
13. A modeler's knife (not shown).

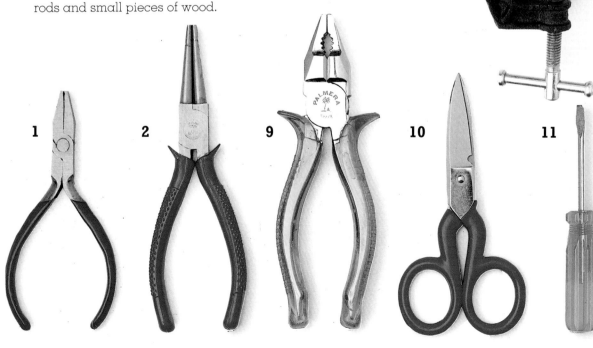

LET'S GET TO WORK

A BELL WITH DIRECT CURRENT

WHAT YOU ARE GOING TO MAKE

You know very well what an electric bell is; your home probably has one that rings whenever someone calls at your front door. But do you know what is inside your doorbell and how it works?

To help you understand this great little invention, we suggest you make a bell that runs on *direct current** from a 1.5-volt battery. Although a house doorbell runs on 110 volts of *alternating current,** yours will work safely with only 1.5 volts, a *voltage** that is harmless because it is low.

After building an electromagnet and a switch—the two main bell components—you will easily understand how an electric bell works.

The top photograph on this page shows our completed bell. However, don't think of our bell as the only model you can make. For all the projects in this book, our illustrations show only one of the many ways your finished devices can look. Our purpose is to give you ideas with which you can have fun and be inventive. We also want to show you how to work with materials you can easily find at home or in your neighborhood hardware store.

THE ELECTROMAGNET

Let's begin with the construction of the bell's electromagnet. This part acts like the mechanism's "motor" as it provides the force for moving the striking device that rings the bell.

An electromagnet is nothing more than a piece of iron (the core), generally a rod, around which has been wound a conducting wire. The wire needs to be insulated to prevent a *short circuit** between the coil and the iron core.

When the ends of the coil are connected to a source of electricity, such as a battery, the iron core behaves like a magnet.

Doesn't this photograph inspire you to build an electric bell?

Test your magnet

Before making the bell's electromagnet, conduct this simple test to see for yourself that what we just explained is true.

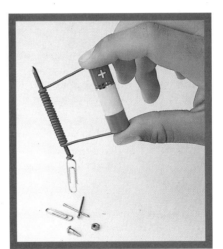

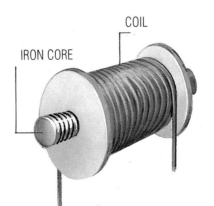

IRON CORE   COIL

Look for a big nail and wind 20 turns of insulated copper wire around it. Strip the insulation from the ends of the wire to expose $^1/_2$ inch (10 mm) of copper wire and place the bare ends in contact with the electrode of a 1.5-volt battery. (Do it with your fingers, as in the photograph.) If you put small iron objects near the nail you'll see how they are attracted by the magnetic force created by the current. An electromagnet is nothing more than a coil of insulated connector wire wrapped around an iron core.

INSTRUCTIONS FOR MAKING THE ELECTROMAGNET

To make the electromagnet for your bell, prepare the following materials:

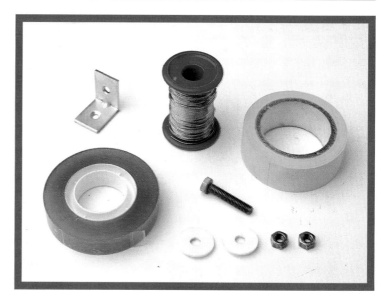

–A 1¼-inch (30-mm) bolt with a ³/₁₆-inch (4-mm) diameter will be the core.
–Two nuts for the bolt. They will hold the electromagnet to an angle bracket.
–An angle bracket, with each side measuring about ⁵/₈ × ³/₄ inch (15 × 20 mm) and having a ³/₁₆-inch (4-mm) diameter hole in the center. We bought the one shown at right from a hardware store. If you want, you can cut yours out of the lid of a discarded tin can (but be careful!).
–Two cardboard (or plastic) washers of a size according to the measurements given in the drawing, at right.
–Enameled copper wire, about 25 gauge (0.5 mm in diameter). Buy a spool of about 165 feet (50 m).
–One roll each of clear tape and insulating tape, white or any color you like.

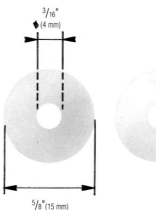

³/₁₆" (4 mm)

⁵/₈" (15 mm)

Above: Materials for making the bell's electromagnet.
Left: Measurements for the cardboard washers.

In making your electromagnet, we suggest that you keep to the sequence of the following procedure:

Begin with the washers

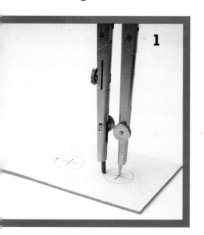 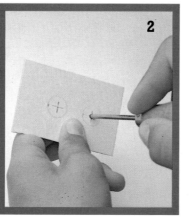 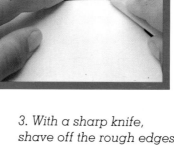 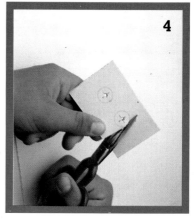

1. On a piece of cardboard or plastic, draw two circles with a diameter of ⁵/₈ inch (15 mm), marking the center of each.

2. Punch a hole exactly in the center of each circle with an awl, slowly widening the hole until it is about ³/₁₆ inch (4 mm) in diameter.

3. With a sharp knife, shave off the rough edges left around the hole by the awl. Do this cautiously to avoid cutting yourself.

4. Cut out the washers with a pair of scissors, being careful to cut on the circular lines you have drawn.

Place the washers on the iron core

Push the bolt, which is to be the electromagnet's core, into the central hole of the two washers, spacing the washers about 5/8 inch (17 mm) apart. Look at the drawing at right, and don't forget to screw on a nut after the second washer.

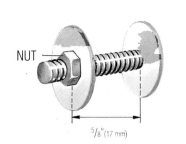

Close-up drawing, showing measurements, of the electromagnet's core where you are going to wind the coil wire.

NUT

5/8" (17 mm)

Attach the core to an angle bracket

The core you have prepared with the bolt and washers must now be attached to the angle bracket. It's easy to do.

SIDE VIEW OF THE COIL MOUNTED ON THE ANGLE BRACKET

NUT

NUT

1. Insert the end of the core into one of the angle bracket's holes and secure it with a nut. It should look like the drawing at far right.

2. Cover the core with a layer of clear tape to prevent the wire that you will wind around it from directly touching the core.

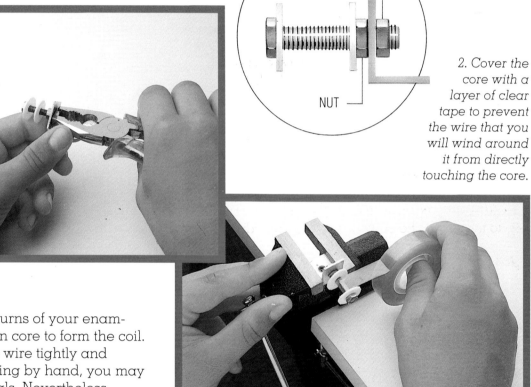

Make the coil

You must wind 200 complete turns of your enameled copper wire around the iron core to form the coil. It is important that you wind the wire tightly and closely together. However, winding by hand, you may find it hard to make perfect spirals. Nevertheless, work carefully and patiently to obtain a sufficiently good (not perfect) coil.

FINISHING END

washer that is near the angle bracket.

INSULATION TAPE

3. When you start winding the coil, be sure to leave a 4-inch (10-cm) piece of wire free before the first turn (starting end), and do the same when winding the last turn (finishing end). Both wire ends should be close to the

4. Finish the coil by wrapping insulation tape around it, as the drawing at right shows.

STARTING END

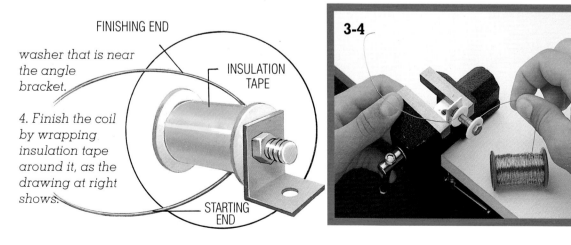

5. Scrape the enamel from about ³/₄ inch (20 mm) of each end of the coil. Use a knife, as shown in the photograph, or sandpaper. It is important to remove the insulating enamel, otherwise the wires won't make electric contact.

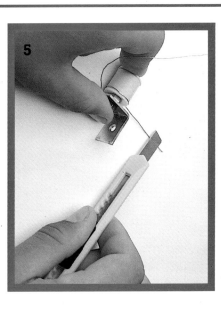

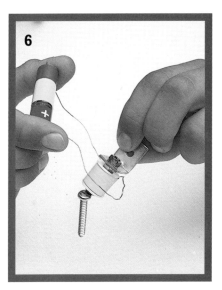

6. Before continuing, check to be sure the electromagnet works. The photograph shows you how, but make certain that the tips of both ends of the coil are free of enamel. If not properly stripped, they won't make good contact with the battery terminals.

Learn to make little "pigtails"!

To make the connecting wires neater and, more important, easier to handle at the connection points, we use a "pigtail" technique. It is easy to learn: Study the photograph at right.

HOW TO MAKE PARTS FROM TIN CANS

For your safety, the cutting procedures that follow should be supervised by an adult.

The bell that you are making calls for various parts that you must cut and shape out of tin from a can. Of course, you can also use a sheet of tin, copper, or brass (from 0.3 mm to 0.5 mm thick) that you can buy in a hardware store.

In our instructions, however, we are assuming you have decided to use a tin can. Be sure to pay attention to the safety precautions we suggest!

–Begin by choosing a good can. The best are those without coatings that are flat, as shown in the photograph. But a large round can (like the ones coffee comes in) is all right, too. Use only the top and bottom.

–Use a good can opener. A dull opener can leave rough edges that can cut your fingers.

–To cut tin you must use a strong pair of scissors designed for cutting hard materials. Electrician's scissors or good kitchen scissors are the most appropriate. Don't use ordinary scissors, you'll break them.

Take your awl, a large nail (or anything similar in shape) and wrap the wire around it so that the spirals touch each other. When you remove the awl, the wire will look like a spring.

–Before you start to cut a piece of tin can, make sure there is no rust. If you see that the can is rusty, throw it away. Don't use it!

–Wear an old pair of leather gloves when cutting the tin. It is the best way to protect your hands.

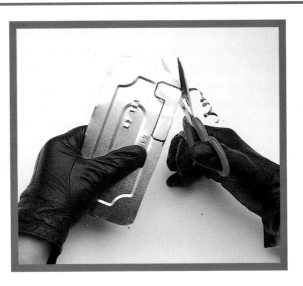

To cut tin safely and efficiently, use an old pair of gloves to protect your hands and the appropriate tool: electrician's or kitchen scissors.

Making the holes

We are going to show you an easy and efficient way to make the holes in the various parts you will be preparing for your bell.

All you need is a hammer, an awl, a rat-tail file, and a flat file. If you have a vise, it will be helpful. But don't worry if you don't have one because all the parts for these projects are small; you can hold them perfectly well with your fingers. Here is the procedure:

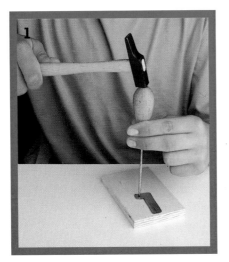

1. Mark the center of the hole on your tin part. Place the part on a block of wood and perforate it using the awl and the hammer.

Place the perforated part on the vise, or hold it with your hand, and widen the hole with the awl.

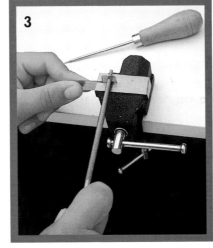

3. When you need a hole with a larger diameter, use the rat-tail file. Insert it in the hole made by the awl, and turn it to file down the hole's border. Stop when you get the desired diameter.

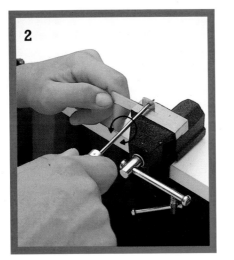

2. Turn the awl right and left—as the arrows in the photograph show—at the same time pushing it through the hole. (Don't go too far!)

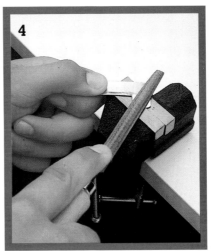

4. Holes made this way always have rough edges on one side. Be careful not to cut yourself! The safe thing to do is eliminate the raggedness with the flat side of your half-round file.

TIN PARTS FOR THE BELL

Now that you know how to do it, let's begin making the parts for your bell.

The drawings, below, give you life-size patterns and show the finished shape of the parts you need. Copy them to a piece of cardboard and cut them out to create a template—or pattern guide—that you can use to trace the shapes on the tin, using a felt-tip pen (as the photo at right shows) or the awl. The broken lines are to show you where each part needs to be bent.

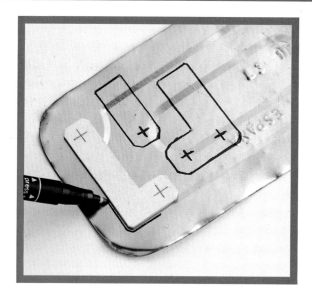

With a felt-tip pen, outline each pattern on the tin. You will then have a clear line to follow when cutting with the scissors.

The scissors will bend the metal as you cut. Flatten the cut parts with a hammer. If necessary, also smooth out the edges with the flat file.

Here are the patterns

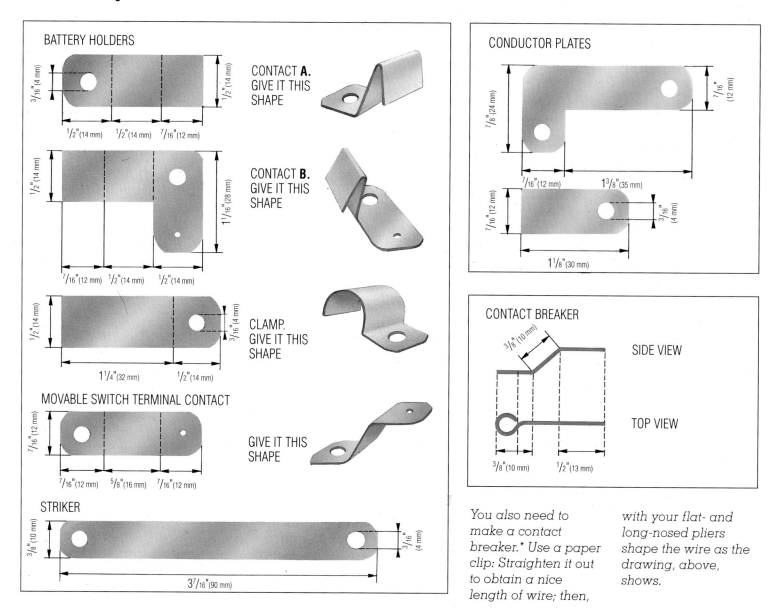

BATTERY HOLDERS

3/16" (4 mm) · 1/2" (14 mm) · 1/2" (14 mm) · 7/16" (12 mm)

CONTACT **A.** GIVE IT THIS SHAPE

1/2" (14 mm) · 1 1/16" (28 mm) · 7/16" (12 mm) · 1/2" (14 mm) · 1/2" (14 mm)

CONTACT **B.** GIVE IT THIS SHAPE

1/2" (14 mm) · 3/16" (4 mm) · 1 1/4" (32 mm) · 1/2" (14 mm)

CLAMP. GIVE IT THIS SHAPE

MOVABLE SWITCH TERMINAL CONTACT

7/16" (12 mm) · 7/16" (12 mm) · 5/8" (16 mm) · 7/16" (12 mm)

GIVE IT THIS SHAPE

STRIKER

3/8" (10 mm) · 3/16" (4 mm) · 3 7/16" (90 mm)

CONDUCTOR PLATES

7/8" (24 mm) · 7/16" (12 mm) · 7/16" (12 mm) · 1 3/8" (35 mm)

7/16" (12 mm) · 3/16" (4 mm) · 1 1/8" (30 mm)

CONTACT BREAKER

3/8" (10 mm) · SIDE VIEW · TOP VIEW · 3/8" (10 mm) · 1/2" (13 mm)

You also need to make a contact breaker.* Use a paper clip: Straighten it out to obtain a nice length of wire; then, with your flat- and long-nosed pliers shape the wire as the drawing, above, shows.

ASSEMBLING THE BELL

You have done the difficult part of the job. Now comes the easy and fun part of this project: Putting everything in its place. But first, you need a few more materials.

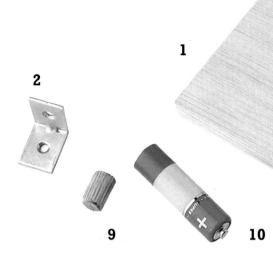

1

2

9 **10**

11

5 **6**

4

3 **8**

7

Besides the electro-magnet and the tin parts you just made, you also need:
1. A wooden base, measuring $3^{1}/_{4} \times 4^{3}/_{4} \times {}^{1}/_{2}$ inches $(80 \times 120 \times 12$ mm).
2. Another angle bracket.
3. Six roundhead, $^{1}/_{2}$-inch wood screws.
4. Two flathead, $^{1}/_{2}$-inch wood screws.
5. A flathead machine screw with a nut.
6. A roundhead machine screw and two nuts.
7. Four washers.
8. Two brass tacks.
9. A wooden dowel.
10. A 1.5-volt battery.
11. A bell cap.

The short conductor plate and the striker

1

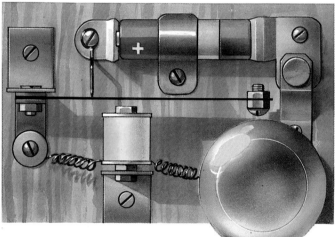

1. The angle bracket will hold the short conductor* plate and the striker. Attach it to the wooden base with a flathead wood screw. But before tightening the screw, slide the short conductor plate under the bracket, and be sure to place the end with the hole facing outward.

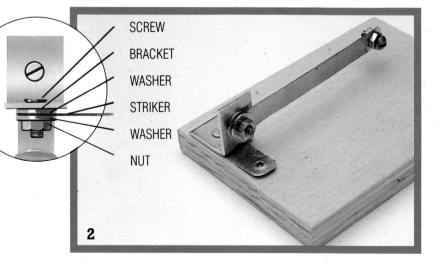

SCREW
BRACKET
WASHER
STRIKER
WASHER
NUT

2

2. Now, let's give the striker a hammer: At one end of it, attach the roundhead machine screw with the two nuts. Next, use the flathead machine screw, a nut, and two washers to mount the other end of the striker to the angle bracket, as shown in the photograph and the drawing.

Battery holder, contact breaker, and switch terminal

1. Screw the battery holder contacts in place. It is important that the space between them be the same as the length of the battery, measured from the positive to the negative electrode. Note: The contact breaker must be mounted to the screw at the same time that you fasten the battery contact that goes nearest the angle bracket. After you screw in the other battery contact, nail a brass tack on top of it, which will serve as the switch's fixed contact.

2. Position the movable switch terminal contact and the long conductor plate. Begin by completing the switch contact with a brass tack and a button made out of a small piece of dowel. Put the brass tack through the small hole in the switch contact and, gently, nail it to the button. The tack's head will act as a contact, while its point will hold the button in place.

3. Now you can mount the switch contact and the long conductor plate. Observe: A single roundhead wood screw fastens both parts. Of course, the tack heads, which make the contact, must have a space between them.

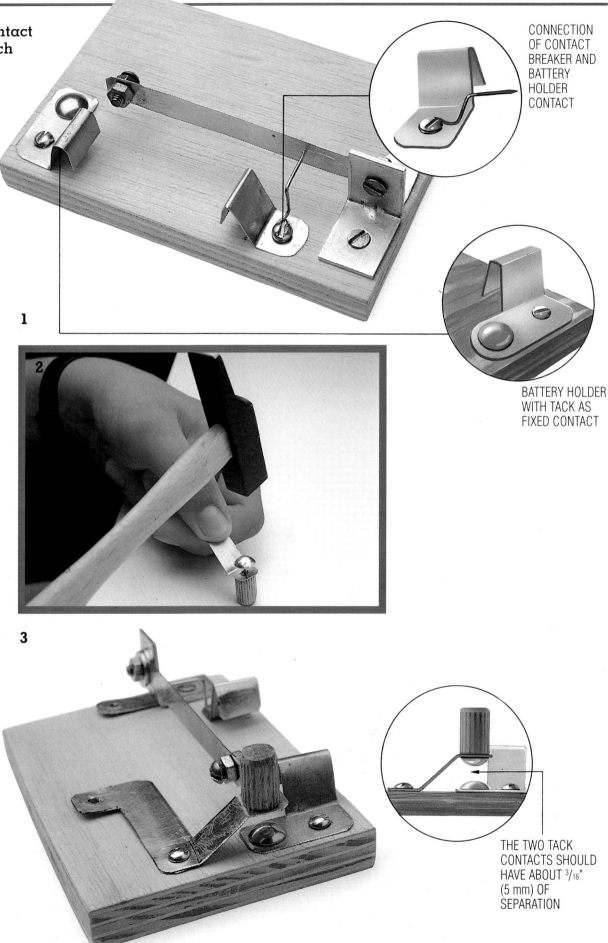

1

2

3

CONNECTION OF CONTACT BREAKER AND BATTERY HOLDER CONTACT

BATTERY HOLDER WITH TACK AS FIXED CONTACT

THE TWO TACK CONTACTS SHOULD HAVE ABOUT 3/16" (5 mm) OF SEPARATION

The electromagnet's connections

Attach the electromagnet you made to the wooden base. Note its position in the photograph and drawing at far right. Then, with a round-head wood screw and a washer, connect each stripped end of the coil to each conductor, as the drawing at near right shows.

WAY TO CONNECT THE ELECTROMAGNET TO CONDUCTOR PLATES

1.5-VOLT BATTERY

STRIKER AND ELECTROMAGNET MUST HAVE A 1/16"-INCH (2-mm) SEPARATION

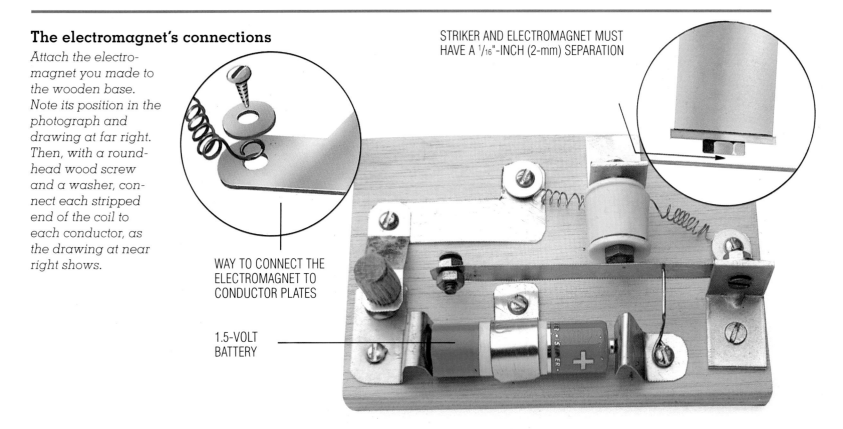

Attaching the bell and the battery

It is hard to say how you should attach the bell to your base because this depends on what type of bell you are going to use. In the photographs below and at right, we offer you two ideas.

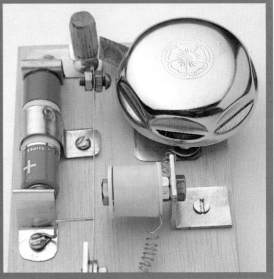

Here, we recycled the cap of a broken bicycle bell.

If you can't find a bicycle bell, you can use the metal cap of any jar, as long as it is not too large in diameter.

EXPLAINING HOW THE BELL WORKS AND TESTING IT

To study *electric circuits** and to understand how they work, technicians use drawings made up of symbols that represent the conducting wires and the different components. These drawings are called diagrams.

Look at the diagram (at right) of the bell you have just made. The names of the components will help you relate the symbols in the diagram to each part of the mounted bell shown in the photograph below.

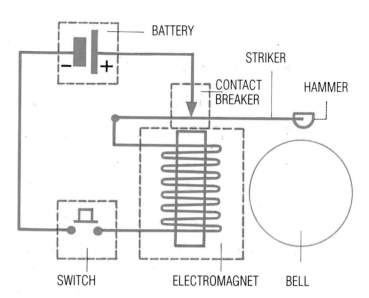

This is a diagram of an electric bell with direct current. As you can see, each component is represented by a symbol.

HOW THE BELL WORKS

We will let our little friend be the teacher on the following page. Look at his explanations and you can arrive at these logical conclusions. Top, left diagram: The switch is open, so there is no current. Top right: Closing the switch completes the circuit, so the magnet attracts the striker, which strikes the bell. As shown in the lower left, this breaks the circuit and turns the magnet off. The striker springs back in lower right, completing the circuit again. Here, we are back at the same position as in the upper right to start over.

Now, let's try it.

TESTING AND ADJUSTING

- When you try the bell for the first time, use a new battery, and preferably one that is alkaline.
- Make certain that there is good contact between the battery terminals and the battery holder contacts.

If you follow the above suggestions and your bell still won't work, check the distance between the electromagnet's core and the striker:

- Failure may be due to too great (or too small) a separation between the core and the striker. You can adjust the distance by adjusting the pressure of the contact breaker on the striker. Decrease the pressure if the separation is too small or increase it if it is too large. As soon as you achieve the right separation you will see the striker move, you will hear your bell ring, and you will shout EUREKA!

When you press the button, current flows through the electromagnet's coil and the contact breaker. The striker hits the bell with the hammer.

Observe: If you don't press the switch button, no current passes through the electromagnet, so it does not work.

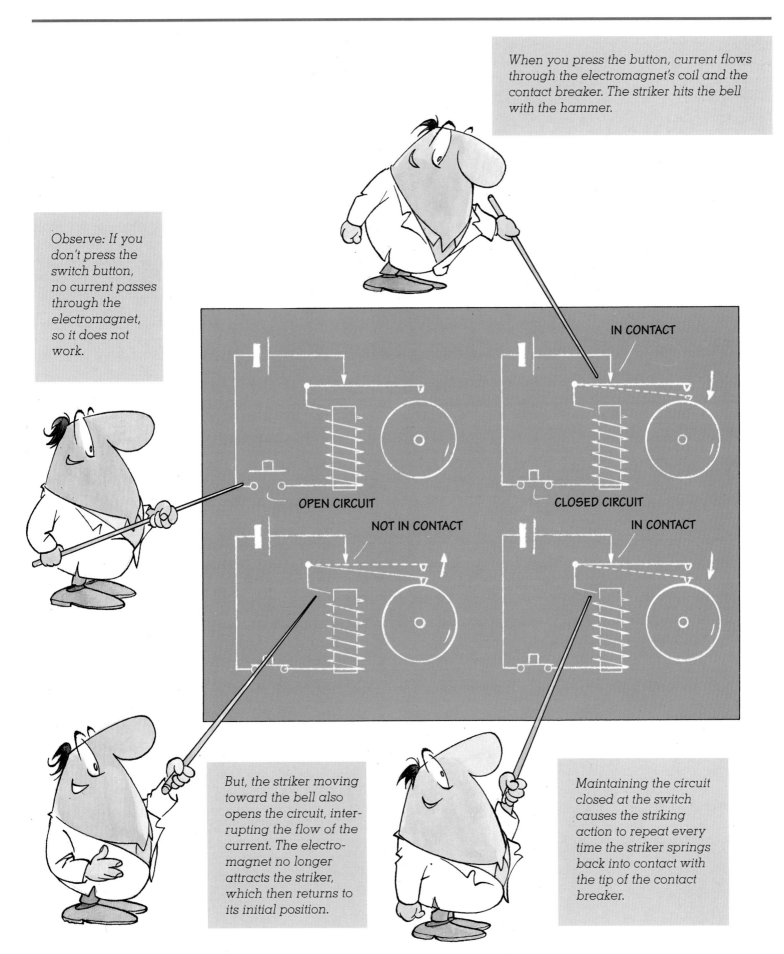

IN CONTACT

OPEN CIRCUIT

CLOSED CIRCUIT

NOT IN CONTACT

IN CONTACT

But, the striker moving toward the bell also opens the circuit, interrupting the flow of the current. The electromagnet no longer attracts the striker, which then returns to its initial position.

Maintaining the circuit closed at the switch causes the striking action to repeat every time the striker springs back into contact with the tip of the contact breaker.

19

AN ELECTRIC BUZZER

WHAT IS A BUZZER?

Briefly, an electric buzzer is a bell without the bell cap.

If you take the cap off the bell you have just made, the striker will continue to move, producing a certain sound: The buzz that any metal strip would make when it is vibrated.

Thus, it is simply a question of modifying the bell's mechanism: Turn the striker into a tongue and make it vibrate with sufficient strength so that the buzz will produce an *acoustic signal.**

THE MECHANISM FOR YOUR BUZZER

As before, we want you to feel free to use any ideas you may have for variations to this model. After all, you could very well produce a device that works better than ours.

However, in this case, do not stray too far from our model, for one practical reason: Our design has a very simple structure that can be used in other more complex devices, which we are sure you will want to make.

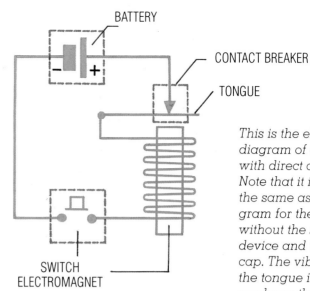

BATTERY

CONTACT BREAKER

TONGUE

SWITCH
ELECTROMAGNET

This is the electric diagram of a buzzer with direct current. Note that it is exactly the same as the diagram for the bell, but without the striking device and the bell or cap. The vibration of the tongue is what produces the sound.

A switch for operating the buzzer at a distance. It is very similar to the bell's switch, but mounted on its own wooden base.

Here you have a photograph of the buzzer you are going to make. It is an uncomplicated setup, considering the experience you have gained with the previous project.

MATERIALS YOU WILL NEED

Some of the materials listed below you can probably obtain from home; the others, from most hardware stores:

1. A 1½ × 2½ × ¾-inch (40 × 65 × 15-mm) piece of wood for the base of the buzzer.
2. Another piece of wood for the switch, 1½ × 2 × ½ inch (40 × 50 × 10 mm).
3. An angle bracket with two equal sides of ¾ × 1¾ (20 × 42 mm), about 1 millimeter thick. Ours has two holes in each side.
4. An angle bracket, with each side measuring ⅝ × ¾ inch (15 × 20 mm) and 1 millimeter thick, with a hole centered in each side. This is the same as the one used for the bell.
5. A bolt with a large head and two nuts. The approximate size of the bolt is indicated in the drawing below.

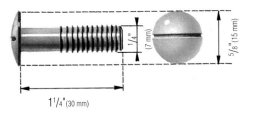

1¼" (30 mm)

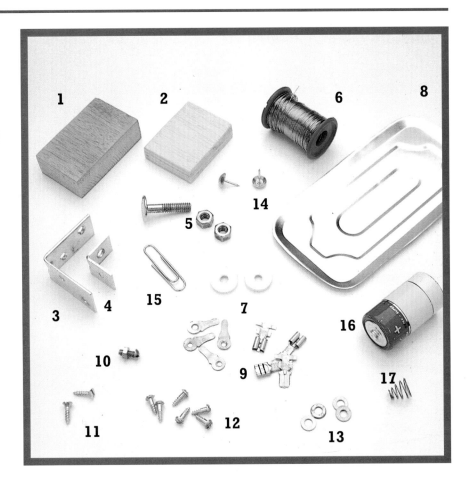

These are the necessary materials for making the buzzer and remote switch.

6. Enameled copper wire, about 25 gauge (0.5 mm in diameter). You will need 33 feet (10 m).
7. Two cardboard or plastic washers for the electromagnet's coil.

¾" (18 mm)

¼" (7 mm)

8. Tin cut from a can.
9. Four *connector terminals*,* the kind called "bayonet lugs."

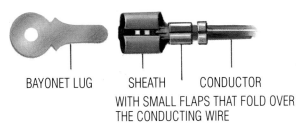

BAYONET LUG

SHEATH   CONDUCTOR
WITH SMALL FLAPS THAT FOLD OVER
THE CONDUCTING WIRE

10. A ½-inch (10-mm) number 8 machine screw and a number 8 nut.

11. Two small flathead wood screws to fit the holes in the angle bracket for attaching it to the wooden base.
12. Six small roundhead wood screws.
13. Four washers.
14. Two brass tacks.
15. A 2¾-inch (70-mm) length of wire, about 1 millimeter thick. As before, you can use the wire from a straightened paper clip.
16. A size C, 1.5-volt cylindrical battery, which measures about 2 inches (50 mm) in length and 1 inch (25 mm) in diameter.
17. A spring for the battery holder. Before buying this, check at home; maybe there's one from a broken flashlight that you can use.

We will guide you, step by step, through the task of assembling your buzzer. However, you already know many of the procedures from having made the bell, so we will not repeat them here.

As you have noticed, the buzzer in the photograph of the previous page does not have the switch mounted on the same base. Its switch is an independent element that is connected to the circuit through wires and connector terminals.

MAKE THE ELECTROMAGNET

Follow exactly the same steps you used in making the electromagnet for the bell. But note the following two modifications:

- The buzzer's coil should have about 250 turns of wire.
- The diameter of the bolt serving as a core is larger than that used for the bell; therefore, one of the holes in the angle bracket may need to be widened. You already know that the rat-tail file is the solution to this problem.

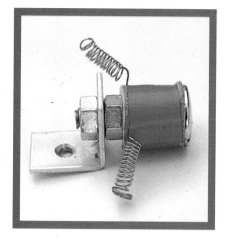

This is the electro-magnet for the buzzer. The coil has 250 turns of wire, and the starting and finishing ends were 7 inches (18 cm) long before they were made into pigtails.

MAKE THE TIN PARTS AND THE CONTACT BREAKER

You need to fashion four parts out of tin for your buzzer. We remind you that you must have adult supervision when cutting the following tin parts.

–Two battery contacts.
–A clamp to hold the battery.
–A tongue to produce the sound.

As those for the bell, the drawings below are actual-size patterns. Use them to make a cardboard template for tracing the shapes on the tin as you did before.

Cut out the parts with electrician's or kitchen scissors (remember to protect your hands), and test your skill in shaping the parts as the drawings show.

BATTERY CONTACTS

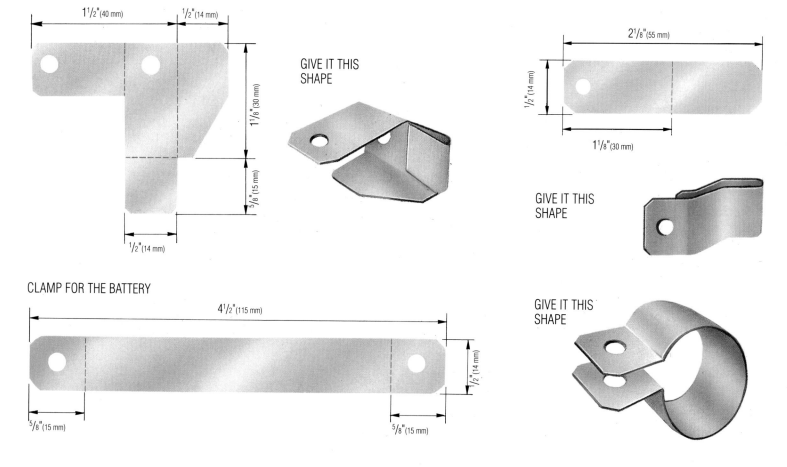

GIVE IT THIS SHAPE

CLAMP FOR THE BATTERY

GIVE IT THIS SHAPE

TONGUE

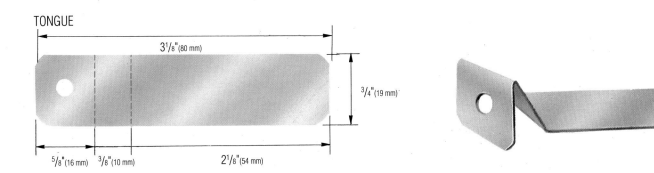

$3^1/8$"(80 mm)

$3/4$"(19 mm)

$5/8$"(16 mm) $3/8$"(10 mm) $2^1/8$"(54 mm)

GIVE IT THIS SHAPE

ASSEMBLING THE BUZZER

After you have made all the parts, mounting them on the wooden base is not very complicated. Do it as the photographs and illustrations show.

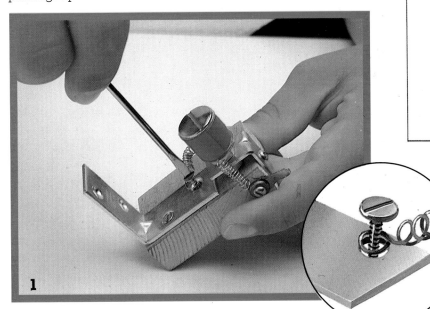

1

$1^1/2$"(38 mm)

$7/16$" (12 mm) $3/8$" (10 mm)

Don't forget to make the contact breaker. You need a total of about $2^3/4$ inches (70 mm) of wire.

1. With a roundhead wood screw, attach the angle bracket that holds the electromagnet to one of the short sides of the wooden base. Then, use the two flathead wood screws to attach the larger angle bracket to the top of the base. Observe: One of the electromagnet's pigtails must be connected to the large bracket with the attachment screw nearest to it. The other pigtail of the electromagnet will be connected to a contact terminal that you will fasten to the side of the base with a roundhead screw and a washer.

2. *It is easy to mount the tongue on the angle bracket. Simply fasten it with a bolt, a nut, and two washers—one in front, the other in back of the bolt.*

2

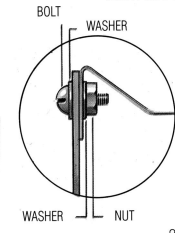

BOLT

WASHER

WASHER NUT

3. The contact breaker, the clamp for the battery, and the contact for the positive battery terminal are all attached to the top of the base with the same roundhead wood screw. Look carefully at the photograph. Here is how: Insert the screw through a washer, then through the eye of the contact breaker, through the holes in both ends of the battery clamp, through the hole of the positive battery contact (making sure the contact wraps around the side of the base) and screw all three parts into the base. Afterward, fasten the positive contact to the side of the base.

4. Push the battery into the clamp until its positive terminal touches the positive contact (A). Now attach the negative contact to the other side of the base, adding a bayonet lug between the contact and the washer (B). As you can see, the electric contact between the buzzer's negative contact and the battery's negative terminal is established through a spring (C). Study the photographs in detail.

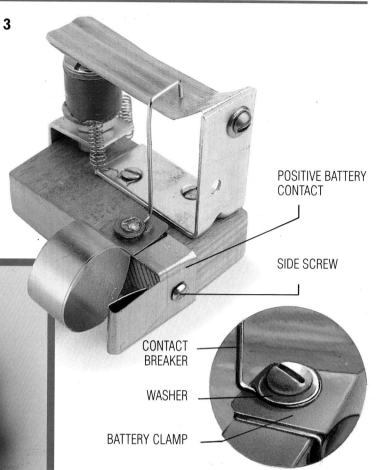

3

POSITIVE BATTERY CONTACT

SIDE SCREW

CONTACT BREAKER

WASHER

BATTERY CLAMP

4

A

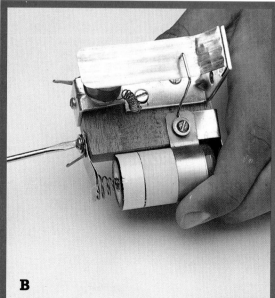

B

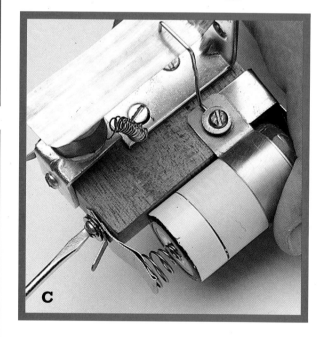

C

Now that you have finished assembling your buzzer, you need a control device that will let you turn it on and off at will.

As is the case with the bell, the control is achieved with a switch.

MAKING THE SWITCH

We are sure that the photograph on page 20 gave you sufficient information to make your switch. Especially since it is almost the same as the switch for the bell.

Nevertheless, at right we show a detailed drawing of the switch, and below the photograph of the entire hookup.

CONNECTIONS BETWEEN SWITCH AND BUZZER

The final hookup is a matter of establishing the connections that complete the circuit between the battery, the buzzer, and the switch, which controls it.

The components in a circuit can be separated by long distances. In our case, however, we are working with a low voltage (1.5 volts), so it is not advisable to separate them too much. If we did, we would create a *voltage drop.** For our purposes, short wires are enough.

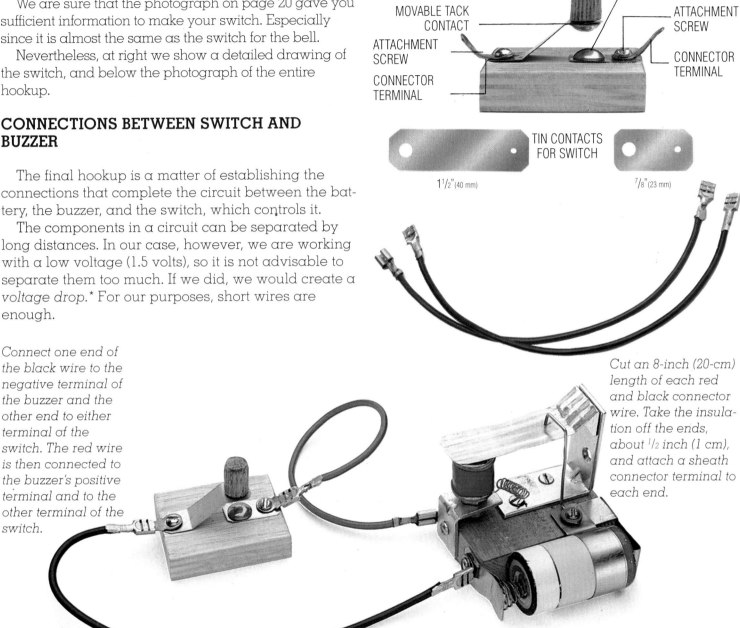

PIECE OF DOWEL — FIXED TACK CONTACT

MOVABLE TACK CONTACT — ATTACHMENT SCREW

ATTACHMENT SCREW — CONNECTOR TERMINAL

CONNECTOR TERMINAL —

TIN CONTACTS FOR SWITCH

1 1/2" (40 mm)   7/8" (23 mm)

Connect one end of the black wire to the negative terminal of the buzzer and the other end to either terminal of the switch. The red wire is then connected to the buzzer's positive terminal and to the other terminal of the switch.

Cut an 8-inch (20-cm) length of each red and black connector wire. Take the insulation off the ends, about 1/2 inch (1 cm), and attach a sheath connector terminal to each end.

THE TEST

When you press the button of the switch to close the circuit, your buzzer's tongue should start to vibrate…at least in theory. It is possible that it will refuse to do so.

If that happens, remember the adjustments we suggested for the bell; they apply in this case, too.

Also, keep the following important details in mind:
- Make sure that there is good contact between the buzzer's contacts and the battery.

- Carefully check the distance between the tongue and the electromagnet. A 1/16-inch (2-mm) separation has given us good results.
- Don't forget to also check the pressure of the contact breaker against the tongue.
- **Be sure to use a new alkaline battery for the test.**

IT'S THE THE IDEAS THAT COUNT!

ATTACH A BUZZER TO INSIDE OF BOX.

A SWITCH TURNS BUZZER ON EACH TIME THE LID IS LIFTED AND OFF WHEN LID IS CLOSED.

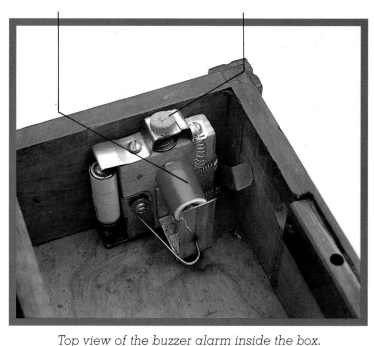

Top view of the buzzer alarm inside the box.

Is our friend hatching an idea?

Well, he is thinking about the possibility of equipping his "treasure box" with an alarm. He is tired of seeing the candy that he keeps in it disappear. Besides candy, his special box sometimes holds other personal and irreplaceable things he wants to keep safe from others.

Making a buzzer like yours has led him to think of a simple adaptation for putting it to good use: as a sound alarm that turns on any time unauthorized hands lift the cover of his treasure box.

And since there should be no secrets between friends, we want to share his idea with you so that you can try it.

ARE YOU READY FOR A CHALLENGE?

AN ALARM

INSTALLATION

You must position the buzzer in the right, front corner of the box. You can fasten it with a screw or with tape—the kind that is sticky on both sides—which is what we used.

The important thing is that the button of the switch stick out above the upper edge of the box. This way, when the lid is closed, its weight pushes the button down, separating the two contacts.

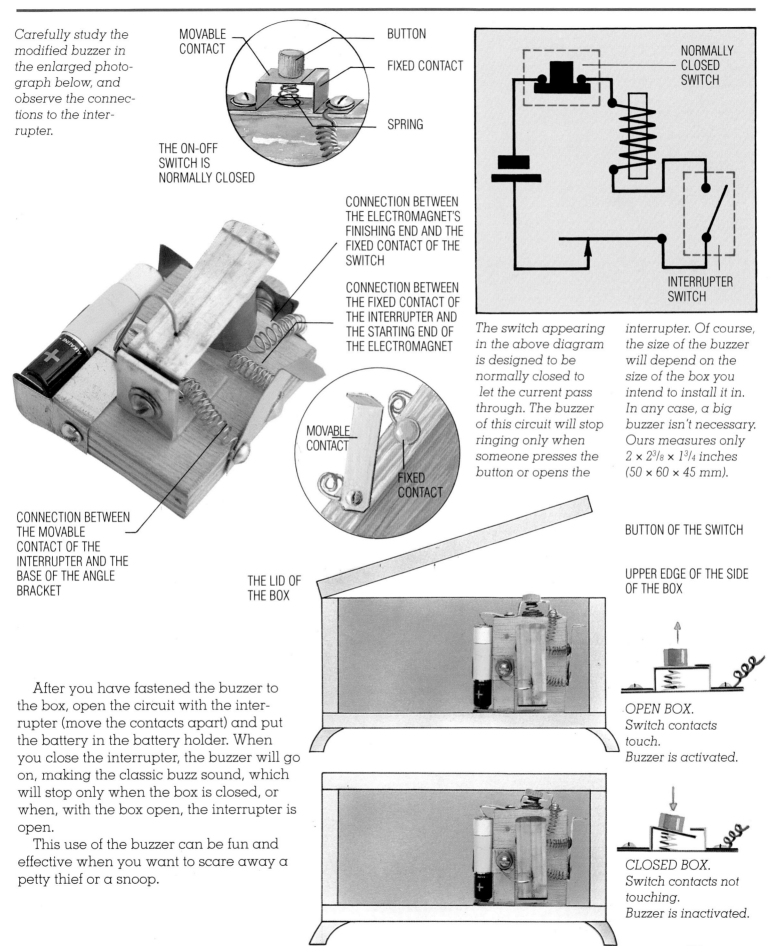

Carefully study the modified buzzer in the enlarged photograph below, and observe the connections to the interrupter.

MOVABLE CONTACT

BUTTON

FIXED CONTACT

SPRING

THE ON-OFF SWITCH IS NORMALLY CLOSED

NORMALLY CLOSED SWITCH

INTERRUPTER SWITCH

CONNECTION BETWEEN THE ELECTROMAGNET'S FINISHING END AND THE FIXED CONTACT OF THE SWITCH

CONNECTION BETWEEN THE FIXED CONTACT OF THE INTERRUPTER AND THE STARTING END OF THE ELECTROMAGNET

MOVABLE CONTACT

FIXED CONTACT

CONNECTION BETWEEN THE MOVABLE CONTACT OF THE INTERRUPTER AND THE BASE OF THE ANGLE BRACKET

The switch appearing in the above diagram is designed to be normally closed to let the current pass through. The buzzer of this circuit will stop ringing only when someone presses the button or opens the

interrupter. Of course, the size of the buzzer will depend on the size of the box you intend to install it in. In any case, a big buzzer isn't necessary. Ours measures only $2 \times 2^3/_8 \times 1^3/_4$ inches (50 × 60 × 45 mm).

THE LID OF THE BOX

BUTTON OF THE SWITCH

UPPER EDGE OF THE SIDE OF THE BOX

After you have fastened the buzzer to the box, open the circuit with the interrupter (move the contacts apart) and put the battery in the battery holder. When you close the interrupter, the buzzer will go on, making the classic buzz sound, which will stop only when the box is closed, or when, with the box open, the interrupter is open.

This use of the buzzer can be fun and effective when you want to scare away a petty thief or a snoop.

OPEN BOX. Switch contacts touch. Buzzer is activated.

CLOSED BOX. Switch contacts not touching. Buzzer is inactivated.

A "MORSE" TELEGRAPH DEVICE WITH LIGHT AND SOUND SIGNALS

A FIRST-CLASS CONSTRUCTION

You are going to undertake the job of building a telegraph, based on the ideas that Samuel F. B. Morse developed during the years 1840 to 1844 when he produced his great invention.

This project involves demanding technical work that will bring credit to whoever does it. Such an ambitious job warrants a few comments.

What does Morse's genius consist of?

As we have said in the first pages of this book,

Morse succeeded in solving the two fundamental problems in long distance communication that existed at that time:

- He developed the ideal "vehicle" for carrying a message over many miles to have it received at the other end.
  As you know, this vehicle was an *electric current** that moved through a conducting wire—the telegraph line—that connected the transmitting office with the receiving office.
- He designed a code made up of letters of the alphabet easily converted into electric impulses of varying duration.

The Morse code consists of assigning each letter of the alphabet a different combination of signals—long signals, which are represented by dashes and short signals, represented by dots.

To estimate the value of Morse's invention, remember that in those days they knew very little about electricity. Electric light had not been invented, and the radio as yet was unimaginable.

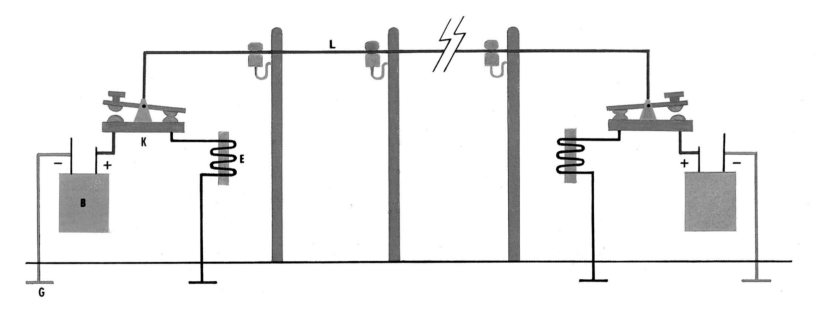

This diagram sums up Morse's idea:
K. Key that provides the electric impulses of different durations to send the message.
B. Electric battery that provides the current.
L. The line of wire through which the impulses, the electric signals, pass.
E. Electromagnet receiver of the signals, the sounder.
G. Ground connection to the ground. In the telegraph installation, the circuit closes through a ground.*

RECREATE MORSE'S INVENTION

We know that you're going to have fun, first, mounting your telegraph device and, later, sharing with another person the possibility of communicating with the dot-and-dash code.

Morse code

First, you need to learn the Morse code, which, as we have just said, is made up of combinations of dots and dashes, and each combination represents a letter of the alphabet or a number.

The box at right shows you part of the international Morse code.

How to "speak" in Morse code

For two people to communicate by using the Morse alphabet, they need only two things:

- To agree on the two signals they're going to use for the dot and for the dash.
- That each signal they send arrive at a receiving end, which implies the existence of a transmitter system.

When the receiver and the sender can see each other, because they are at close range and because there is nothing blocking their vision, it is easy to find many ways of "speaking" Morse. Just use your imagination.

Morse with gestures

In my childhood, a friend and I had a secret system for communicating with each other.

All we needed to put our system into action, was to be able to see each other's left hand. We had learned Morse code and used it to send our signals. We agreed that the sending transmitter would be our left hand: With our outstretched hand, palm down, and with our thumb held steady next to the other fingers. To fold the index finger downward meant "one dot"; to fold all four fingers, "one dash." Easy, right?

a	• —		n	— •
b	— • • •		ñ	— — • — —
c	— • — •		o	— — —
ch	— — — —		p	• — — •
d	— • •		q	— — • —
e	•		r	• — •
f	• • — •		s	• • •
g	— — •		t	—
h	• • • •		u	• • —
i	• •		v	• • • —
j	• — — —		w	• — —
k	— • —		x	— • • —
l	• — • •		y	— • — —
m	— —		z	— — • •

1	• — — — —		6	— • • • •
2	• • — — —		7	— — • • •
3	• • • — —		8	— — — • •
4	• • • • —		9	— — — — •
5	• • • • •		0	— — — — —

end of transmission   • — • — •
call   — • — • —

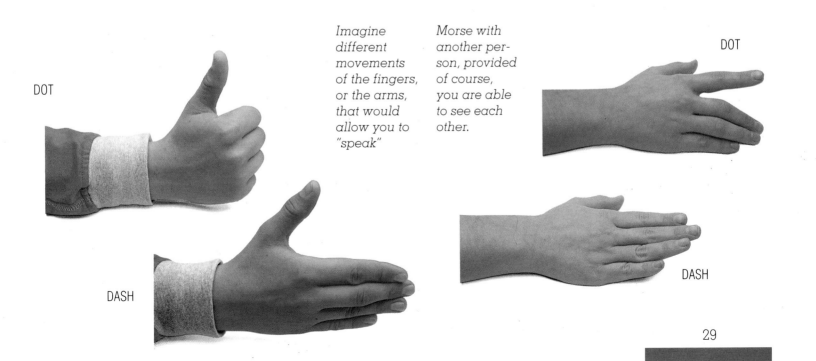

DOT

DASH

Imagine different movements of the fingers, or the arms, that would allow you to "speak"

Morse with another person, provided of course, you are able to see each other.

DOT

DASH

Morse with light signals

Any system that allows us to produce light flashes of different duration can be used to send Morse messages. All you have to know is:

Short flash = dot
Long flash = dash

Many battery flashlights are able to produce flashes. Besides a normal switch, they have a button that will let you practice Morse with light signals. It is an easy system two people can use at night to communicate over a distance, if atmospheric conditions allow it, and if nothing interferes with the light from their flashlights.

MORSE TELEGRAPH WITH SOUND SIGNALS

Sound is also a good way to communicate in Morse:

Short sound = dot
Long sound = dash

A whistle, a flute, a harmonica...whatever makes a sound will permit you to "speak" Morse, over short distances.

What about long distances? How will we manage to get the sound to the receiving end? Blowing desperately?

Nowadays, we have available two easy solutions: the telephone and the radio.

But suppose we don't have either of these methods, as was the case with Morse. Is there another way?

As you already know, the first telegraph built by Morse is a system that converts electric impulses of different duration (dots and dashes) produced by the sender's transmitter into sound signals, which, in turn, are produced in the receiver's device.

How is this achieved?

That is what you are going to learn while you make a telegraph which, naturally, won't be like the "professional" ones. However, even with its technical limitations, your telegraph will function as did Morse's primitive transmitter-receiver units.

You are going to have fun, you'll see.

TWO HELPFUL TIPS

1. As you can imagine, to communicate over a distance with someone, you are going to need two transmitter-receiver devices; one for each "telegraph operator." Therefore: **You should make duplicates of each of the parts described in the following pages.** Or you can work with a friend who can make the second set of parts, while you work on the first set.

2. Look ahead now at our second suggestion in the caption at the bottom of page 41. To save time, you can do that work before undertaking the assembling procedure that is described in pages 36 through 40.

As we have done previously, we provide you with a photograph of the transmitter-receiver you are going to make. We hope that seeing it beforehand will inspire you to roll up your sleeves and get ready to work.

LET'S GET TO WORK

You are going to assemble a Morse transmitter-receiver that will function with either sound signals or flashing-light signals. As we always do, we'll begin by listing the necessary materials.

MATERIALS YOU WILL NEED

We are not including what is needed to make the telegraph's buzzer because it is the same as the one you already made.

Besides the buzzer, you need:

1. Thirteen ½-inch, number 8 roundhead wood screws.
2. Washers for the screws.
3. A piece of plywood, 7 × 7 × ½ inches (180 × 180 × 10 mm).
4. Two wooden buttons made from a dowel.
5. A ⅛-inch (3-mm) thick piece of plywood. A strip at least 4 inches (10 cm) long.
6. Six sheath connection terminals.
7. Six bayonet lug connection terminals.
8. Two brass tacks.
9. A sheet of tinplate or a large quantity of tin from cans.
10. Red connector wire, about 4 inches (100 mm).

11. Red and black connector wire, 6 inches (150 mm) of each.
12. A miniature 4.5-volt lightbulb.
13. The plastic body of a used-up felt-tip pen.
14. A small container of contact cement.
15. A 4.5-volt flat battery.
16. The plastic cap of a spray can.
17. A socket for the miniature lightbulb that has connecter terminals.
18. (Not shown) Three number 10 hex nuts; one brad (thin nail), 1½ inches (40 mm) long.

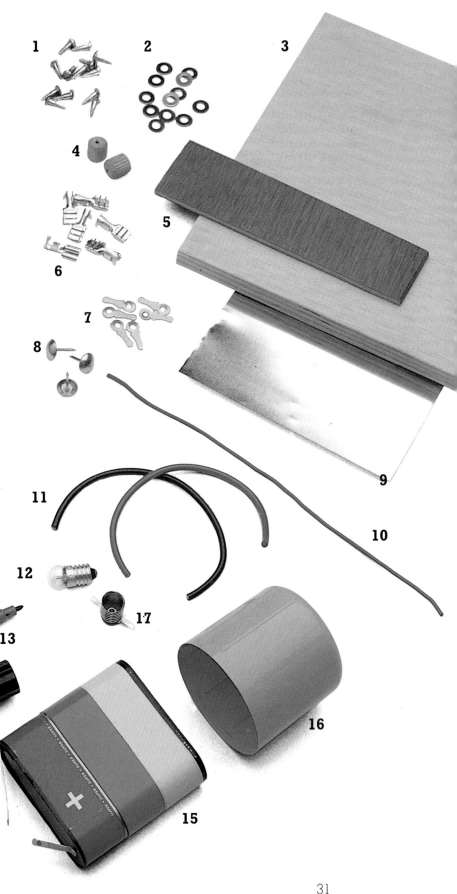

THE TIN PARTS

Under adult supervision, begin with the most tedious job: Cutting the tin parts that you are going to need for establishing the path for the electric current. Some are flat plates and others will need a specific shape.

Because you already know how to do this, we won't repeat our instructions. Here you have actual-size patterns of several parts.

Remember that if you first make a cardboard template of all the parts, it will be much easier to draw their shapes correctly on the tin.

CONTACTS FOR THE BATTERY
Diameter of the holes = $^3/_{16}$"(4 mm)
You need two contacts exactly the same

PIECE TO HOLD THE BATTERY

CONDUCTOR PLATES
Diameter of the holes = $^3/_{16}$" (4 mm)

Plate 1

MOVABLE CONTACT FOR THE SELECTOR SWITCH

Plate 2

Plate 5

Plate 3

Plate 4

The lengths of the conductor plates have to be as indicated on this page, so they will fit on the 7 × 7-inch (180 × 180-mm) base. The width can vary a little.

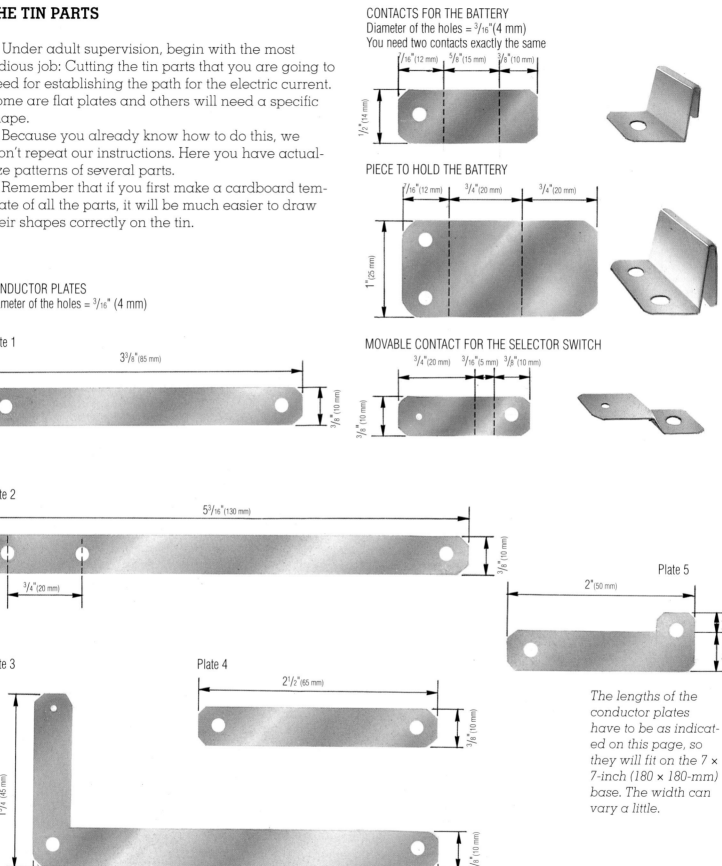

CONSTRUCTION OF THE TRANSMITTER

In the construction of the sending key you also need parts made of tin that we haven't included in the previous list because they are more difficult to construct and require detailed instructions.

We will describe them one by one; but note that the drawings that follow are not actual size.

THE BAR

This part is made with:
1. A strip of wood.
2. A plate of sheet metal, which covers the underside of the bar.

1. The wooden strip

You can easily cut a strip from a $^1/_8$-inch (3-mm) thick piece of plywood. If the wood is a little thicker, it doesn't matter, although it will be more difficult to cut.

2. The conductor plate

Be precise when making this part: The straight lines must be straight and the measurements exact. We suggest that instead of tin, you use a piece of copperplate. Copper is softer than tin, and it is a better conductor of electricity.

You must cut out a part (of copperplate, tin, or brass, 0.3 millimeter thick), following the shape and measurements you see in the drawing, at right.

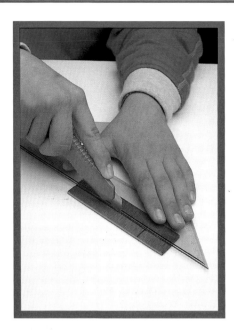

On the plywood, draw a $^1/_2$ × 4-inch (14 × 100-mm) rectangle. If the wood is $^1/_8$ inch (3 mm) thick it will be very easy to cut the rectangle with a modeler's knife (WATCH YOUR FINGERS!) and a ruler. If it is thicker, it will be harder to cut, but you can do it by going over the cut several times with the knife.

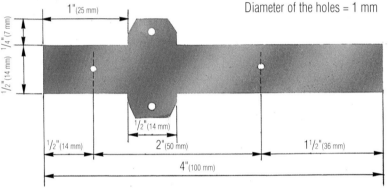

Diameter of the holes = 1 mm

1"(25 mm)

$^1/_4$" (7 mm)

$^1/_2$"(14 mm)

$^1/_2$"(14 mm)

$^1/_2$"(14 mm)

2"(50 mm)

$1^1/_2$"(36 mm)

4"(100 mm)

JOINING THE TWO PIECES

Now you need a little contact cement. Read the instructions for its use and follow them to the letter.

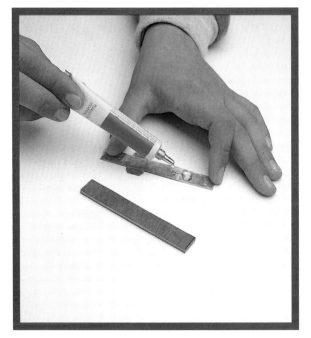

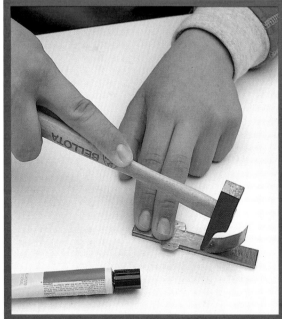

Apply a few drops of cement to one of the sides of the wood. Before it dries, use a finger to spread the cement uniformly over the surface to be glued. Do the same with the metal part. When the cement on both pieces is dry, line the pieces up perfectly, with the cemented sides face to face. Then, press one piece against the other. You can do it as shown in the photograph, with the narrow part of a hammer pressing down along the metal.

ADDING THE CONTACTS AND BUTTON TO THE KEY

The sending key has two contacts: One in front and the other in back. The one in front is made with a ½-inch, number 8 wood screw and two number 10 nuts that slip over the screw as spacers. The rear contact is the same, except that it uses only one nut. The bar of the key has two small holes on the metal side to receive the screws.

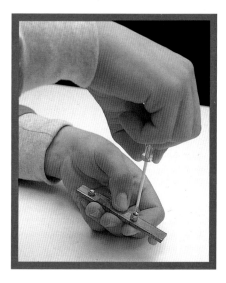

Put the nuts in place and screw the wood screws into the holes. You can see their placement in the drawings below.

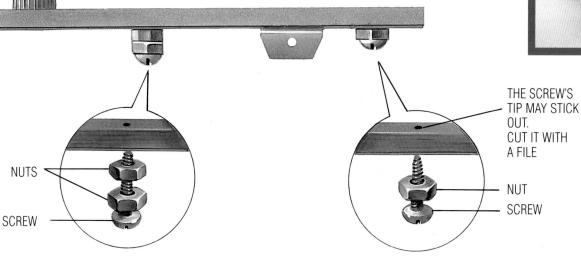

NUTS

SCREW

THE SCREW'S TIP MAY STICK OUT. CUT IT WITH A FILE

NUT

SCREW

Side view of the key bar with contacts and button in place. The button is glued to the bar's upper side near the front edge, with contact cement.

THE KEY'S FIXED CONTACTS AND THE SUPPORT

Cut the contacts and the support for the key's bar from tin (as always, with adult supervision). Follow the measurements and shapes shown in the enlarged drawings. As you can see, the rear contact is the hardest to make because it must be shaped to support the bar as well. But, with patience, it won't be a problem for your already skilled hands.

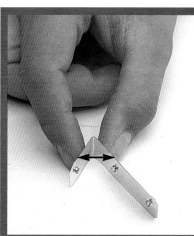

From tin, cut out the rear contact and make the three holes that you need. Draw a line halfway between the two holes that are further apart. Fold the tin at this line until the two holes touch face to face.

REAR CONTACT AND KEY SUPPORT

Diameter of the holes = ³/₁₆" (4 mm)

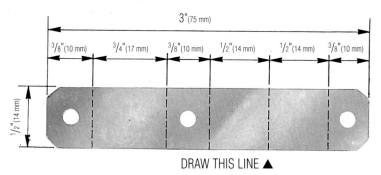

3" (75 mm)

³/₈" (10 mm) ³/₄" (17 mm) ³/₈" (10 mm) ½" (14 mm) ½" (14 mm) ³/₈" (10 mm)

½" (14 mm)

DRAW THIS LINE ▲

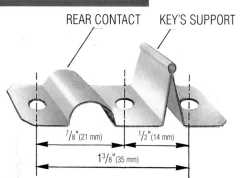

REAR CONTACT   KEY'S SUPPORT

⁷/₈" (21 mm)   ½" (14 mm)

1³/₈" (35 mm)

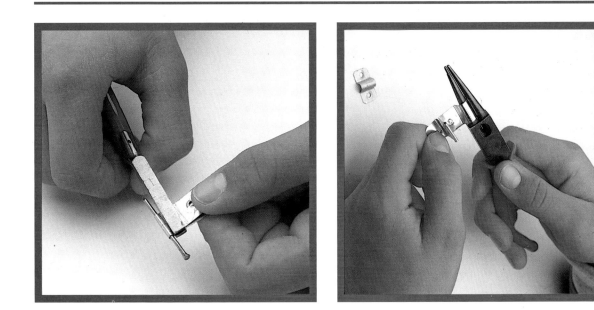

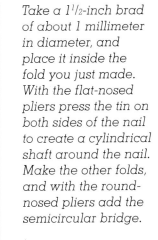

Take a 1¹/₂-inch brad of about 1 millimeter in diameter, and place it inside the fold you just made. With the flat-nosed pliers press the tin on both sides of the nail to create a cylindrical shaft around the nail. Make the other folds, and with the round-nosed pliers add the semicircular bridge.

As you can see by the drawing at right, the other fixed contact is easier to make than the first. Besides, you now have experience having made similar parts. Now, cut this contact out of your tin and make the holes and a semicircular bridge centered between those holes.

For the key's bar to return to its original position every time it is pressed down, you must add a flexible metal strip that will act as a spring. You can fashion this part using the long brass electrode of a spent 4.5-volt battery. Brass is more flexible than tin.

MOUNTING THE CIRCUIT

You have the buzzer, and you have finished preparing all the other parts of the circuit for your telegraph. You are ready to begin mounting it.

1. MODIFICATIONS TO THE BUZZER

- Remove the battery's clamp and the two contacts.
- Also remove the terminal that attaches one end of the coil to the wooden base.
- Reattach the contact breaker, which has become loose, and at the same time add a connector terminal.

Your buzzer should now look similar to the one in the photograph at right. Set it aside for now. You won't be mounting it until later.

FIXED FRONT CONTACT FOR THE KEY
Diameter of the holes = ³/₁₆"(4 mm)

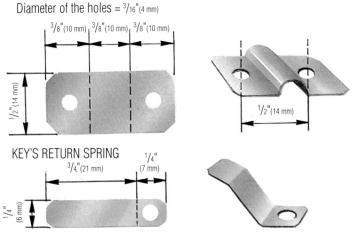

³/₈"(10 mm) ³/₈"(10 mm) ³/₈"(10 mm)

¹/₂"(14 mm)

¹/₂"(14 mm)

KEY'S RETURN SPRING

³/₄"(21 mm) ¹/₄"(7 mm)

¹/₄"(6 mm)

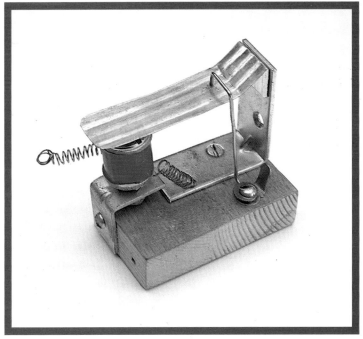

Your modified buzzer must look like this before you add it to the circuit.

2. CONNECTING THE CONDUCTOR PLATES

Use the full-size illustration, below, as a guide. This bird's eye view shows the wooden base with all the conductor plates and necessary terminals mounted in place and properly connected.

Note the following:

- *You must maintain certain distances.*
- *It is important that distance B, between the front and rear contacts, be the same 2-inch (50-mm) distance that separates the contact screws on the underside of the key's bar.*
- *Observe that 12 of the screws have washers. They help to provide better electric contact.*

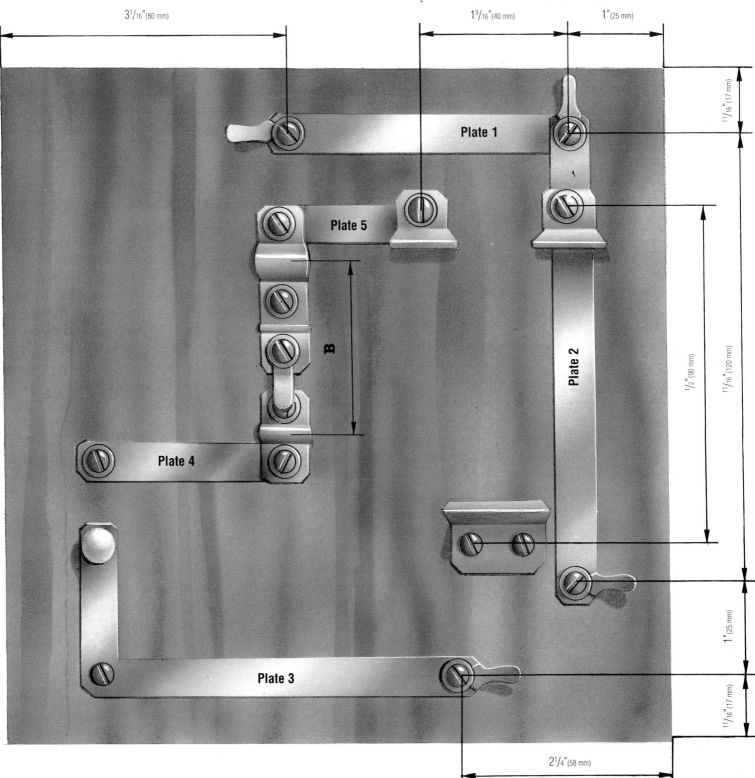

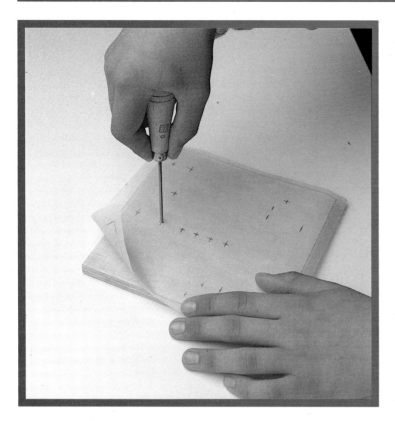

3. MOUNTING THE BUZZER AND THE SELECTOR SWITCH

First, attach the buzzer to the base as the drawing at right shows.

You can use one of the following methods:
- With contact cement. (You already know how to do this.)
- With mounting tape that is sticky on both sides.

Next, assemble and mount the *selector switch**:
- As you have done previously, add the button and tack contact to the movable contact, and add a tack to the fixed contact.
- Then, connect the movable contact to conductor plate 4, using a screw and two washers. (Study the detailed drawing, at right.) Remember that the movable contact should be able to turn, so don't overtighten the screw.
- Finally, mount the second fixed contact for the selector switch, which, as you can see in this drawing and photographs that follow, is another brass tack to which one of the buzzer's coil pig-tails will be connected. You must position this tack alongside conductor plate 4, but at a distance that will place it directly under the movable contact's tack when the selector switch is turned to meet it.

PREPARING THE BASE

The photograph, at left, and the caption, below, will help you prepare the wooden base.

Put a piece of wax paper on our drawing on the previous page. Trace the edges of the base in the drawing and the location of each screw. Then, put the pattern on your wooden base and use an awl to punch holes to receive the screws. If you cut the tin parts with the measurements we have given you, the holes on the base should line up with those of the parts for mounting.

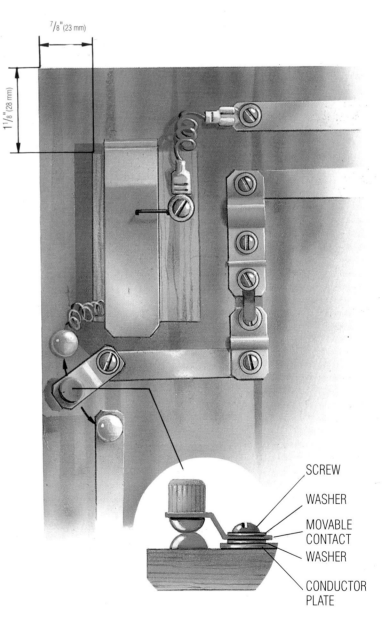

7/8" (23 mm)

1 1/8" (28 mm)

SCREW

WASHER

MOVABLE CONTACT

WASHER

CONDUCTOR PLATE

PUTTING THE KEY IN PLACE

Your wooden base now has the contacts and the support shaft for the key's bar. The support shaft will allow the bar to pivot every time you press down with your finger to transmit a dot or a dash. All you need to do now is secure the bar to the support.

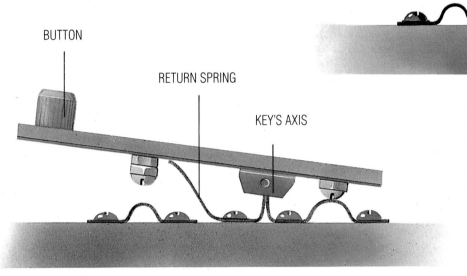

BUTTON

RETURN SPRING

KEY'S AXIS

Above: This side view shows the contacts positioned in front of the buzzer. They include the support shaft (which receives the axis of the bar) and the return spring for pushing the key back up after you press it down.

Left: The same contacts with the key in place. The axis on which the key pivots is the same brad you used to form the shaft of the support, remember? You can see it in the first photograph of page 35.

The photograph, at right, shows how to mount the key on its support:

It is just a matter of lining up the holes in the bar's metal flaps with the shaft's openings, and pushing a nail through the first flap, the shaft, and the second flap.

Now, with a small hammer, you can tap the nail gently about ¹/₂ inch (1 cm) into the base of the buzzer.

As you know, the key's axis is a 1¹/₂-inch (35-mm) brad with a diameter no bigger than 1 millimeter.

After pushing this nail through the bar's flap holes and the support shaft, it must be partly hammered into the base of the buzzer, approximately ¹/₂ inch (1 cm).

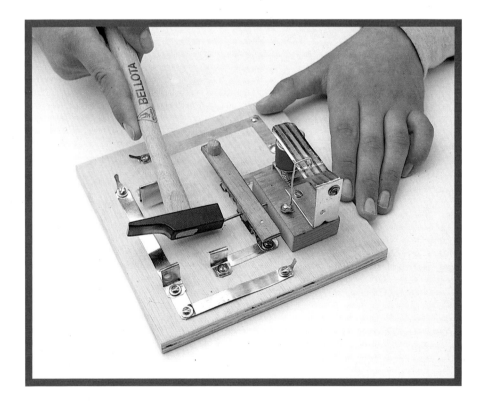

THE LIGHT SIGNAL TRANSMITTER-RECEIVER

At the beginning, we explained that your Morse telegraph would be equipped to transmit and receive both sound and light signals.

Well, the time has come to build the light signal transmitter-receiver. Of course, all you really need is a simple miniature lightbulb and socket hookup that can be connected to the proper conductor terminals.

However, we think you are going to prefer the more imaginative device we suggest on this page.

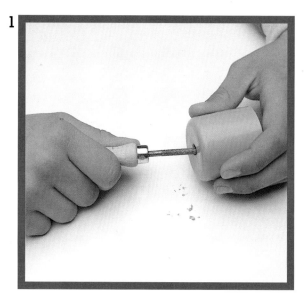

1. Take the plastic cap (from a spray can) you are going to use and make a hole in the center of its base. CAREFUL! The diameter of this hole must be just wide enough to receive the lightbulb's socket.

Carefully widen the hole with the rat-tail file.

2. After testing the hole with the socket for a proper fit, fashion an attachment flap for the support you are going to make next. Study photograph 4, at right, and the bottom photograph on page 41. Be inventive! After everything is in place, screw the lightbulb into the socket; now you have a spotlight.

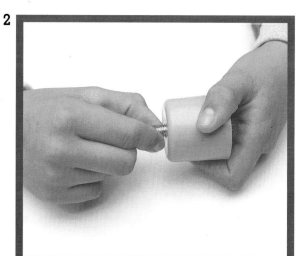

4. Insert your attachment flap into the support you have just made. Connect the upper terminal of each wire to one of the lugs of the lightbulb socket. Your spotlight is ready to send or receive light signals in Morse code.

This is one idea. Do you have others? Perhaps you want to use different materials.

3. Empty out the body of a dried up felt-tip pen. With adult supervision, use a modeler's knife to cut two notches in the sides, wide enough to allow each one of the 6-inch (150-mm) lengths of connector wire mentioned in the materials list to pass through it. Then, put a sheath connector terminal on each end of the two wires.

THE LAST CONNECTIONS

Your telegraph is almost complete. Very soon you will have the satisfaction of seeing the results of your expert work. First, however, a few last connections are necessary to ready your device for the initial test that will tell you whether it works the way it should.

Do the following:

1

1. Take the 4 inch (100 mm), red connector wire called for in the materials list. On each end of this wire, attach a sheath connector terminal. (You already know how to do this.) Next, make a pigtail with this wire (another task with which you are familiar).

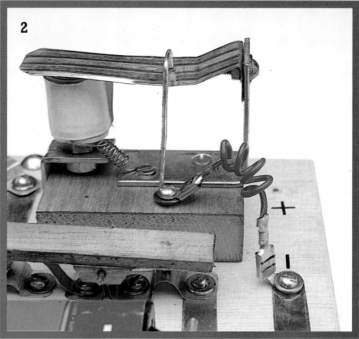

2. Connect one end of the pigtail you have just prepared to the contact breaker terminal at the base of the buzzer. The other end must be connected to the terminal of the conductor plate that in photographs 2 and 3 is marked with a minus sign (–).

After all the connections are made, position the battery. To insure that the battery's electrodes will make good contact with the tin terminals, bend the electrodes as shown in the photograph, below.

3

3. Secure the light on the wooden base and connect the sheath terminals from the light's two wires to the bayonet lugs of the conductor terminals nearest to them. Study the photograph, above.

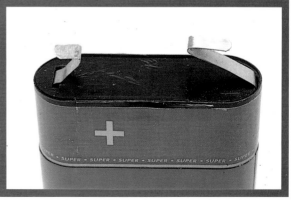

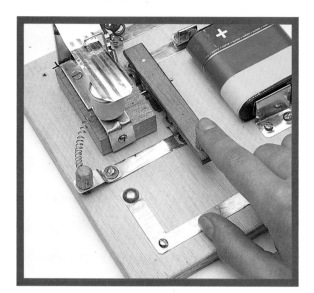

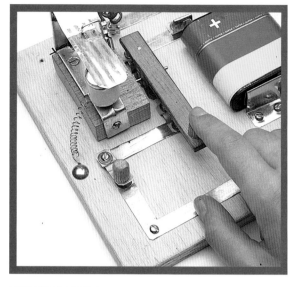

With the switch, select the "sound" position (left photograph) and push the button on the sending key. With each tap, the buzzer will sound out your signal. Remember: a short sound is a "dot," a longer one is a "dash." Next, select the "light" position (right photograph). Each time you press the key, your spotlight will light up: a quick flash means a "dot"; a slower one, a "dash."

TESTING THE DEVICE

Everything is ready for the big test. You already know that the buzzer works because you tried it before. You also made sure that the signal light works. Right?

If something goes wrong at this point, then, you can probably assume that it is a bad connection. On the other hand, the buzzer's contact breaker may have shifted during remounting and may not be making contact with the tongue of the buzzer. As the photographs above show, make a double test. One with the selector switch in the "sound" position; the other with it in the "light" position.

FINISHING DETAILS

Your Morse telegraph is complete, and it works. However, if you want the satisfaction that comes with a job nicely finished, include the two details explained in the caption of the photograph at bottom.

1. Using white cardboard, make a cover for the battery. Next, glue a photocopy of the Morse code chart on the cover. If you don't know the code too well yet, the chart will be a big help to you when you play "telegraph operator." 2. Paint your telegraph unit with the two colors that you like most. Use a quick-drying paint, such as latex. You may have already done this, as we suggested on page 30. Otherwise, you must first disassemble and then reassemble your device. But we guarantee that the result will make you feel proud.

CREATING A TWO-WAY TELEGRAPH LINE

In the previous pages we guided you through the construction and testing of a telegraph transmitter-receiver. However, as we already explained, a telegraph installation requires at least two devices connected by a line, which makes the two-way transmission of messages possible. This means that it is necessary to make another transmitting-receiving device exactly like the one you have just mounted.

If you followed our advice, you already have the two transmitting-receiving units. Now, you and your "partner" can easily hook up the necessary telegraph line.

Preparing the line connections

Before you can establish a connection between the two devices, you need to make a few modifications to both units:

1. As the left photograph at bottom shows, add a bayonet lug to the conductor terminal to which the contact breaker of the buzzer is hooked up (1).

This becomes the negative terminal.

2. Put another bayonet lug under the screw and washer that hold the movable contact of the selector switch (2, in photograph).

3. Add a double bayonet lug terminal to the wooden base (3). Position it as shown in the photograph. One of the lugs will act as the positive terminal.

4. Prepare an 8-inch (20 cm) length of connector wire by adding a sheath terminal at each end.

Turn this wire into a pigtail and connect one end to the movable contact of the selector switch (2); connect the other end to the double terminal you just added (3).

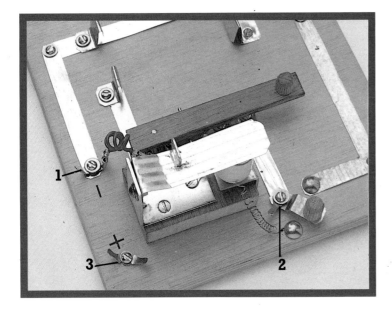

This photograph clearly shows the three new terminals that are necessary to connect a two-way telegraph line.

Here is the pigtail connected to the movable contact of the selector switch (2) and to the positive terminal (3).

For terminal 1, above, to be negative and terminal 3 to be positive, the battery must be positioned exactly as shown in photograph 3 of page 40.

Of course, if you position the battery the other way around, the telegraph will still work. But the *polarity** will be different and, consequently, the direction of the current will change.

The telegraph line

To establish your telegraph line, you need two conducting wires. You can buy cable that consists of red and black conducting wires attached to each other. If you use wire of only one color, mark the ends of the wires so you can distinguish which ends are connected to the positive terminals; and which, to the negative terminals of the devices. The ends of each wire take sheath connector terminals.

Test

Before installing your telegraph, test the connections. But position the two transmitter-receivers fairly close—one at each end of a table, for example.

- Connect the wires to each device making sure that positive and negative terminals are properly matched at both units.
- The position of the selector switch—light or sound—in each unit will dictate which signal is activated whenever the sending key is pressed down. With both units set for sound, sound signals will be transmitted and received. But you can have them set differently, which allows, for example, one operator to send light signals while the other operator receives sound signals.

terminal; the red, to the positive.

Separate the wires for approximately 4 inches (10 cm) at both ends of the cable. Put a terminal on each of the four ends. To keep the wires from separating beyond the desired length, bind the cable with a few turns of insulating tape.

Red and black cable is ideal for working with direct current. The black wire is connected to the negative

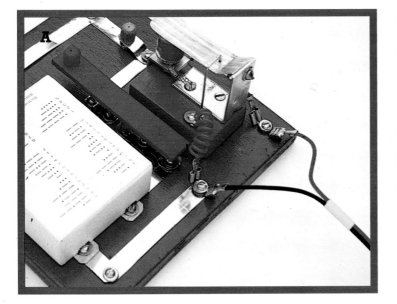

Note: The wire hookups on device A have the same polarity as those on device B. Don't forget: Red wires are connected to the positive terminals; black, to the negative.

Now, look at the selector switch of device A. Because it is set in the "light" position, even if device B were to be transmitting sound signals (with its switch set in the "sound" position), device A would receive light signals. In other words, both operators can choose their own incoming or outgoing signal. It is also possible to transmit signals with the switch open. In this case, the sender does not hear or see the signals he or she is transmitting. This is not recommended, because you won't know whether you are making any errors.

LONG-DISTANCE INSTALLATION

The distance between your two transmitter-receivers cannot be very long. Remember that you are working with only a 4.5 voltage; thus, too long a distance would cause a drop in voltage that would weaken the signal.

Besides, it would cost too much money to buy so much conducting cable.

A length of 65 to 80 feet (20–25 m) of line is plenty for:

- Communicating between two rooms in the same house.
- Communicating between two apartments in the same building: with the neighbor on the side, or the one above or below.
- Communicating between two rooms in different houses, face to face on a normal narrow street...and other possibilities you will surely discover.

From here on, it is up to you to figure out the best way to install the line between your telegraph "office" and that of your business partner, if you have one.

Also, if you have balconies or windows from which you can see each other, don't overlook the possibility of communicating only with light signals. This way you won't need a line and will avoid the risk of disturbing a neighbor with the noise of the buzzer.

ARE YOU READY FOR A CHALLENGE?

Is there something you can do to strengthen a signal weakened by too long a line?

If your line produces a drop in voltage, the solution is to add another 4.5-volt battery connected in a series with the other one. Hook it up as you see in the photograph below. You will notice that the signals received on each device are much stronger.

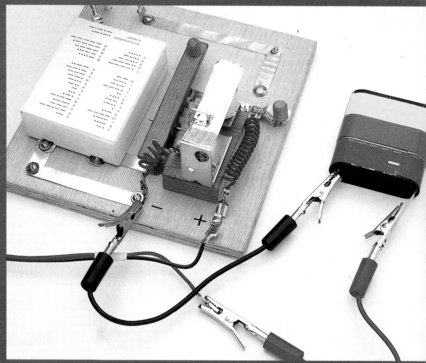

On one of the devices, connect the positive end of the line to the negative electrode of the new battery. Then, connect the positive terminal of the new battery to the negative terminal of the circuit. The voltage of the new battery will thus be added to that of the first two batteries in the circuit.

COMBINATIONS OF BATTERIES

Let's clarify what we mean by connecting batteries in a series.

Batteries can be combined in a *series connection* or a *parallel connection*. Study the diagrams at bottom and the captions at right; they will help you understand each connection.

Parallel connection: The electrodes of two or more batteries are all connected positive together with positive; and negative, with negative. If the batteries are each 1.5 volts, the combination is still only 1.5 volts, but it can produce three times as much current.

Series connection: Two or more batteries in a combination where the positive electrode of one is connected to the negative electrode of the one that follows. In this connection, the voltage of all the batteries are added up.

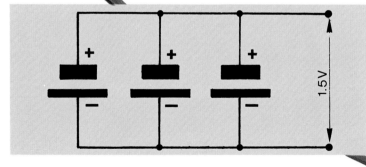

PARALLEL CONNECTION

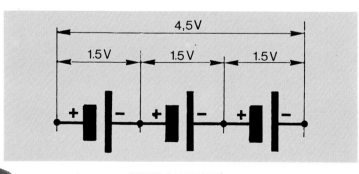

SERIES CONNECTION

GLOSSARY

acoustic signal. A sound that the ear can perceive. Acoustics is the branch of science that studies sound.

alternating current. An electric current that in a circuit flows in one direction and then reverses that direction. The number of cycles that an alternating current passes through in a time interval (one second) is known as the frequency. It is measured with a unit called hertz (Hz), which is equal to the frequency of one cycle per second. (See illustration below.)

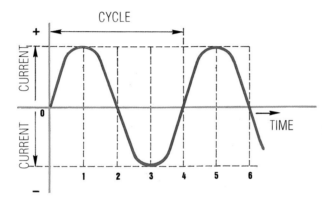

Graph of an alternating current. The curve between point 0 and the 4 on the Time axis is what is known as the cycle of the current. During a cycle, the current has all the possible values between a positive maximum and a negative maximum.

conductor. A material that allows electricity to flow through it. Tin, copper, and other metals are good conductors of electricity.

connector terminal. A small component used in electricity and electronics for easily establishing electric contact between conductors or between a conductor and an electric device.

contact breaker. A point making electrical contact with an armature that vibrates as the contact is alternately made and broken.

direct current. A current in an electric circuit that always flows in the same direction. (See illustration on bottom of page.)

electric circuit. The circular path through which an electric current flows from a power source to a device and back again.

electric current. The flow of electricity through the conductors of a circuit. An electric current can be *alternating* or *direct*.

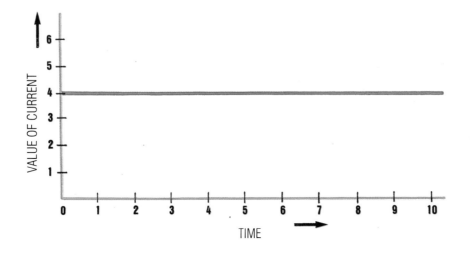

Graph of a direct current. Because the current maintains the same value at every time interval, its graphic line runs parallel to the Time axis.

flint. A hard, quartz-type rock that can be broken and shaped if struck in the right place. In prehistoric times, humans used flint to make their first tools (spears, knives, axes).

ground. In certain electric circuits, the connection made between a terminal and the ground, which acts as a return path for the current. (See illustration below.)

Primitive radio receivers needed a ground.

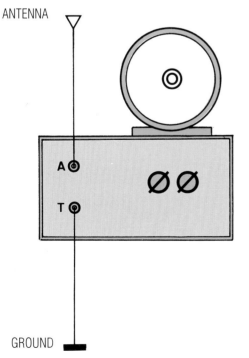

ANTENNA

A

T

GROUND

mile. A unit of distance in the system of measure used in Great Britain, the Commonwealth countries, and the United States. Its equivalent value in the metric system is 1,609 meters.

polarity. In electricity, this refers to the electrodes of a generator or the terminals of an electric circuit with direct current, according to the direction of the current. The current comes out of the positive electrode or terminal and returns into the negative electrode or terminal. (See illustration below.)

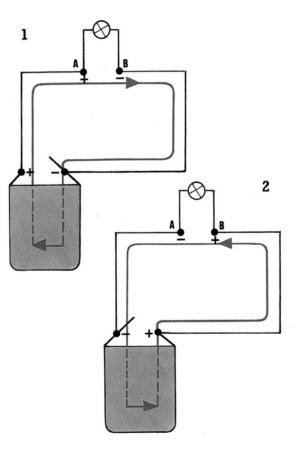

The positive electrode of a generator (such as a battery) is that from which the current flows out; the negative electrode, that to which the current returns after traveling through the circuit. The terminals of the devices connected to the circuit will carry the same polarity as that of the generator. Above, in diagram 1, terminal A is positive and B is negative. In diagram 2, the polarity is reversed: Terminal A is negative and B is positive.

47

With the movable contact of the switch in position 1, lightbulb A goes on. With the contact in position 2, lightbulb B turns on.

selector switch. An electric control device that opens to interrupt the current in a circuit and closes to allow it to flow. More complex switches are made to direct the current into selected circuits. (See illustration below.)

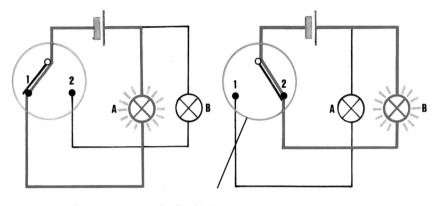

TWO-POSITION SWITCH

short circuit. A shortcut that occurs in the path of a current when the input and output ends of a circuit make electric contact. This results in an abnormal increase in the intensity of the current that could burn out all or part of a circuit.

voltage. The level of electric energy measured in volts that is present between any two terminals of a circuit. It is also called potential difference or electromotive force (emf). (See illustration on right.)

voltage drop. A reduction in voltage of an electric current that occurs between two ends of the conductors. This results from the resistance that the conductors offer to the passing current. The longer the conductors are, the greater is the reduction.

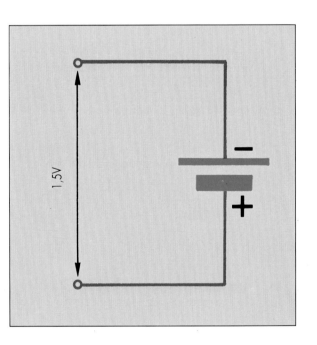

The voltage, potential, or electromotive force between the two electrodes of a battery is measured at 1.5 volts (V).